SELECTED POEMS OF LAWRE

Selected Poems of
LAWRENCE DURRELL

Edited by
PETER PORTER

faber and faber

First published in 2006
by Faber and Faber Limited
3 Queen Square London WC1N 3AU

Photoset by RefineCatch Ltd, Bungay, Suffolk
Printed in England by TJ International Ltd, Padstow, Cornwall

A CIP record for this book
is available from the British Library

ISBN 978-0-571-22739-6
0-571-22739-2

2 4 6 8 10 9 7 5 3 1

Contents

Introduction

The chance to make a selection of the best poetry of an important but somewhat neglected poet serves this compiler as an occasion for a public display of repentance. I have always been an enthusiastic lover of Lawrence Durrell's poetry, but not long ago I committed a minor slight on his reputation. I wrote the entry on Durrell in *The Oxford Companion to Twentieth Century Poetry*, edited by the late Ian Hamilton and published in 1994. Although I find my short account of his verse largely accurate, it now seems to me I did not properly evaluate his power and originality. Worse than this, I was tempted into one of these 'soundbites' we scatter in our entries in encyclopaedias. This in turn was picked out by the blurb writer to the volume for emphasis on the jacket. When looking at the *Companion* recently I was shocked to find these words: 'Durrell was to prove more a Mendelssohn than a Mozart: his poetry did not mature and produce the masterpieces his readers had every reason to expect from such youthful achievement.'

There is a small amount of ungenerous truth in this statement, but it is so wincingly knowing and derogatory I am glad to be able to turn against it now. Not that being any sort of Mendelssohn is a minor achievement; but disclaimers come in comparatives, and this was an unworthy one. The Mozart reference was also an easy get-out. Who would claim for anyone the gifts Mozart possessed? But Mozart and Mendelssohn are apposite enough in one sense. Durrell shared with them (and in poetry with Pope, Keats and Heine) an early burgeoning of talent, an almost Minervan springing fully-armed into maturity. He was like Auden in that his movement from worthy but clumsy romantic verse into a recognizable self-style happened so suddenly. His *Collected Poems 1931–1974*, the definitive recension complied by James A. Brigham in 1980, reprints a stack of poems dated up to 1934, and so written mostly before he was twenty-one, which, with the best will in the world, nobody could say were striking. Turn a page and you encounter the sequence 'The Death of General Uncebunke'. The change is one of the most palpable transformations in contemporary poetry. I shall return in a short space to the originality of this sequence but for the moment harp on how original and immediately recognizable Durrell's talent was when it was launched. The three most remarkable first collections of poetry in modern times in the English-speaking world seem to me to be Wallace Stevens's *Harmonium* (1923), *Poems* by W. H. Auden (1930) and Durrell's *A Private Country* (1943), but Stevens was forty-four when he burst (if that's the right word) on the scene. Auden was younger than Durrell at his debut but he had already built up a formidable reputation as an undergraduate at Oxford and was being spoken of very quickly as 'the new guy who's got into the landscape' (Wyndham Lewis). Since *A Private Country* did not appear until 1943, Durrell's precocity must be predated to the latter part of the Thirties, when many of its poems were written. To publish your first collection at the age of thirty-one is not particularly precocious but to be producing masterpieces at first emergence certainly is.

Durrell arrived virtually unannounced, and perhaps in consequence he was not seen as Messiah material. He had no university credentials but belonged to a species of colonial-administrator family usually absorbed effortlessly into the British home establishment. Though sent from India to school in Britain by his parents he did not acclimatize to his homeland, at least in his younger days. Members of his family, while fully English by education, preferred to live in more exotic places.

Lawrence as a young man is presented picturesquely in his brother Gerald's books about the family's life in Corfu. Gerald went on to be a celebrated animal curator and his brother to exhibit a lifelong fondness for the bohemian and extravagant, especially in various countries of the Mediterranean. This affection for what might be described without injustice as Romanticism is the reason both for many Puritanical literary critics' suspicion of him, and for a more clear-sighted conviction that his capacity to elevate the highly coloured and the picturesque to a plane of serious beauty and decorum is his greatest gift as a poet.

Before *A Private Country* Durrell was equipping himself with the technical and imaginative skills which that initial volume so strikingly asserts. He was living a peripatetic existence very different from that characteristic of poets of the time. His name is seldom found in the many roll-calls of English poets of the Thirties, either of the politically committed or of those consciously opposed to the Auden full-fruit standard. His loyalties were with the writers of Greece who still lived in ways informed by the Classical past, and with the defiantly bohemian and sexually implicit chroniclers, such as Henry Miller, whom he got to know in Paris. One of his own productions of this time is an icon of the genre popular among writers of the unpolitical Thirties, the authors of 'banned books', fugitively issued and much in demand among expatriates, pornographic autobiographies. His *Black Book* (1938) is a true product of the private and libertine presses in Paris, though it is less sexually direct than the works it pays homage to: Henry Miller's *Tropic* Books (of *Cancer* and *Capricorn*). *The Black Book* is more truly a harbinger of the brilliant poetry of *A Private Country*, but without the fiercer scatalogical overtones. Later in this introduction it will be necessary to face the question of whether Durrell abandoned poetry for prose, since today readers usually point to the Alexandria and Avignon sequences of novels if Durrell's name is in question. *The Black Book* is a piece of diablerie but it previews the brilliant vernacular juxtapositions of his poetry written at the same time. It edges into the diffuse though always tangible world of Surrealism. The Surrealist Movement was a literary phenomenon more than a pictorial one only in France. Dalí, Max Ernst and Kurt Schwitters come to mind as painters, but poets such as Paul Eluard, Pierre Reverdy, Benjamin Peret, Max Jacob and Robert Desnos are the real Surrealists. These men produced a remarkable harvest of serious and original poetry and should be distinguished from publicity-seekers like the self-elected leader of the movement, André Breton. I am not suggesting that these men were a direct influence on the early Surrealist-tinged poetry of Lawrence Durrell, merely that *A Private Country* and the two volumes which succeeded it, *Cities, Plains and People* (1946) and *On Seeming to Presume* (1948) contain the only body of poetry within the English-speaking world at that time which can be considered alongside the Surreal works of the Frenchmen listed above.

Surrealism cast a pallid shadow over English life in the Thirties and Forties. Its only acknowledged champions were David Gascoyne, Hugh Sykes-Davies and Philip O'Connor. Gascoyne was appointed by public opinion the style's chief apologist in Britain chiefly for making himself known in Paris and for having written a tame introduction to Surrealism. His true talent was for lyrical introspection, as his wartime poetry revealed. Sykes-Davies dipped an academic toe into Surrealism and little more. Philip O'Connor, whose strange pieces were one of the delights of Geoffrey Grigson's *New Verse*, was an impressive experimenter but might be called Surrealist only because no other label quite fits him. Durrell did not welcome any particular label, and indeed in *Uncebunke* went out of his way to avoid any classification. *The Death of General Uncebunke, A Biography in Little*, to give it its full title, is prefaced by the words: 'Not satire but an exercise in ironic compassion, celebrating a simplicity of heart which is proof against superiority or the tooth of the dog . . . After all, we may have had other criteria, but they were only criteria.' Why then speak of Surrealism? The proof of the pudding is in the eating, not the labelling. This extended fantasy is both a moving homage to the Empire-builders Durrell grew up among but whom he abandoned, especially in the certainties they held about the absolute verities, and also a recognition that language is most itself when it approaches the finite world in playful mode. If the Auden Group of poets were co-opting Marxist terms to provide them with an analysis of a world in crisis (and everyone of any shade of opinion seems to have felt that this indeed was what was happening in the run-up to the Second World War, a decade which inherited the full economic weight of the Depression), then Durrell was entitled to call on the many dream-worlds which Freud and psychoanalysis had been declaring for years were the true groundbase of European life. It was Durrell's genius to relate this non-rational pressure to the surface world his generation had inherited, while paying tribute to the lyricism of more traditional ages. *Uncebunke* is divided into fourteen carols, which celebrate and lament the family and career of a typical imperial servant of England. The irony is gentle but it is underlain by a scathing sense of loss of purpose and direction. The long history of English expansion is shrunk to a set of exhibits in a Cabinet of Curiosities. At the poem's beginning, the General is mourned: he is addressed as Uncle:

> My uncle sleeps in the image of death.
> In the greenhouse and in the potting-shed

The wrens junket: the old girl with the trowel
Is a pillar of salt, insufferably brittle.
His not to reason why, though a thinking man.
Beside his mesmeric incomprehension
The little mouse mopping and mowing,
The giraffe and the spin-turtle, these can
On my picture-book look insufferably little
But knowing, incredibly Knowing.

Straight after this introduction comes an account of
Uncebunke's picaresque career in overseas service, his adven-
tures being half the sort which litter military and diplomatic
memoirs, and half Lewis Carroll-like bizarre inventions. Then
Durrell introduces the second important family member, Aunt
Prudence.

Aunt Prudence, she was the eye of the needle.
Sleeping, a shepherdess of ghostly sheep.
'Thy will be done in Baden Baden.
In Ouchy, Lord, and in Vichy.'
In the garden of the Vicarage sorting stamps
Was given merit of the poor in spirit
For dusting a cinquefoil, tuning the little lamps.

Well, God sends weather, the English apple,
The weeping willow.
Grum lies the consort of Prudence quite:
Mum as a long fiddle in regimentals:
This sudden IT between two tropical thumbs.
Unwrinkle him Lord, unriddle this strange gorgon,
For tall Prudence who softens the small lamps,
Gives humble air to the organ that it hums.

The poem from this point alternates reports of Uncle and
Aunt in turn – the masculine stanzas beginning either 'My

uncle sleeps in the image of death', – or 'My uncle has gone beyond astronomy', and the feminine less strictly prefaced but always starting with Prudence's name, by way of a key signature.

> Prudence plays monumental patience by candles:
> The puffins sit in a book: the muffins are molten:
> The crass clock chimes,
> Timely the hour and deserved.
> Presently will come the two welcome angels
> Noise in the hall, the last supper be served.

This is Surrealism of the domesticated sort, reminiscent of the formal pictures of Dorothea Tanning. For all the dislocations of narrative, it is never merely smart or chic. Nor has it any flavour of apocalypse. The whole of *Uncebunke* makes an interesting comparison with Auden and Isherwood's play *The Dog Beneath the Skin*, in particular that work's finale at a patriotic rally in the village of Pressan Ambo, a rural cross-section of England very like the setting of *Uncebunke*. These two poets, disimilar in most respects, have the measure of the England of their childhoods – part caricature, almost of a *Punch* cartoon, part recognition of incipient Fascism – yet carried out with a sort of retrospective love. Durrell, the expounder of Mediterranean light and classicism, and Auden, historic transplant to America, honour the country of their birth throughout their poetry, though each testifies continually to his inability to live there.

The 'Five Soliloquies from the Tomb of Uncebunke' continue this vein but are largely superfluous to the characterization. If nothing in the later poetry is as fantastical as *Uncebunke*, the tone established early stayed with him for the rest of his poetry-writing life. As late as 1969, in a revision of a poem set originally in Paris in 1939 entitled 'Solange', we catch the comical shifts and kaleidoscopic instances characteristic of *Uncebunke*. This poem is difficult to print excerpts from, but section No. 6 is included in this book.

After the fanfares of *Uncebunke*, the places described and the scenes of their development shift from the rueful England he had etched so carefully to the domain which he was to make his own, the Mediterranean, especially its eastern shores. The second and larger part of *A Private Country* consists of an assortment of poems inspired by Greece and points east of Greece. For all of Durrell's familiarity with the area, the poetry he devotes to these parts shares with the English and American expatriate poets of the nineteenth century a conscious sense of interpretive skill rather than of total identification. Durrell seems to have been born with a sense of the continuous history of the Ancient World, and like so many Northern Europeans, he felt compelled to go on pilgrimages to the cradle of Western civilization. Fortunately, he never allowed the contemporary world of the Levant, whatever its debasement, to be obscured by the classical past. His poetry honours an ideal world, perhaps indeed an imaginary world, but it is continuously annotated by modern life in the very sites of its ancient greatness. His poetry gives chapter and verse to that perennial European nostalgia for the vanished classical world. Like Schiller via Schubert, he cries, '*Schöne Welt, wo bist du?*' Poems such as 'At Epidaurus', 'Nemea', 'On Ithaca Standing', 'Letter to Seferis the Greek' (I have preferred to include the much later poem entitled simply 'Seferis'), 'Alexandria' and 'Poggio' shine as brightly as the Ionian Sea or the chips of unfading mosaic in the temples and palaces of the Ancient World. They are romantic but not deceived. In his novels, and to a lesser extent in his travel books, which became his major preoccupation, Durrell was to yield to the temptation to exaggerate the glamour of the Eastern Mediterranean, and to go further and shock his readers with ever more outrageous detail of sexual and social imbroglio, but this was a prose habit – his poetry remained centred on the reality of Greece, Egypt and Italy.

His great achievement in this vein is 'On First Looking into Loeb's Horace', This is a poem of a highly original order. The title immediately suggests a postmodern reordering of Keats's famous sonnet, but Durrell is more conscientious than most poets who play with the retreading of past masterpieces. It is a love poem into which is folded an indirect narrative and an excellent example of literary criticism. Critical assessment is always more attractive written in the form's own medium – that is, verse itself. The poet finds a copy of the Loeb Edition crib of Horace's poetry annotated by a former lover's hand. Reading along with her comments he analyses the Roman poet's life and work. Not only has the love affair perished, but its loss is matched by the vanished Mediterranean civilization which nurtured Horace and still inspires today's readers of Latin literature. Durrell's handling of the interweaving of these themes is an unprecedented way of composing a dramatic lyric. Unprecedented, but the ghost of Robert Browning does look out from the lines:

> I found your Horace with the writing in it;
> Out of time and context came upon
> This lover of vines and slave to quietness,
> Walking like a figure of smoke here, musing
> Among his high and lovely Tuscan pines.

There follows an analysis of Horace's timid and doubting nature and its equally obsessive concern for the beauty of the Italic landscape and the fastidious management of its farms and estates. The fifth stanza brings back the plot of the lover's involvement, as she writes in the margin.

> Here, where your clear hand marked up
> 'The hated cypress' I added 'Because it grew
> On tombs, revealed his fear of autumn and the urns',
> Depicting a solitary at an upper window
> Revising metaphors for the winter sea: 'O
> Dark head of storm-tossed curls'; or silently
> Watching the North Star which like a fever burns
> Away the envy and neglect of the common,
> Shining on this terrace, lifting up in recreation
> The sad heart of Horace . . .

That sad heart kept the Roman poet close to the cruelty built in to the beauty he recorded:

> Easy to be patient in the summer,
> The light running like fishes among the leaves,
> Easy in August with its cones of blue
> Sky uninvaded from the north; but winter
> With its bareness pared his words to points
> Like stars, leaving them pure but very few.

Behind these lines, Horace's own poetry shines, especially his *Odes* and in particular Book I No. 4, '*Solvitur acris hiems*'.

The speaker tells us very little of his relations with the woman whose annotations he had expanded but as the poem addresses the character of Horace the reader becomes aware of an equal sadness in the lost love of the contemporary man and woman. The parallelism of the melancholy the Loeb volume arouses is finely controlled. The poem ends with a kind of double dissolution:

> So perfect a disguise for one who had
> Exhausted death in art – yet who could guess
> You would discern the liar by a line,
> The suffering hidden under gentleness

And add upon the flyleaf in your tall
Clear hand: 'Fat, human and unloved,
And held from loving by a sort of wall,
Laid down his books and lovers one by one,
Indifference and success had crowned them all.'

Another high point in Durrell's preoccupation with the classical world is his poem 'Alexandria'. This is a homage of a special sort, one tamed by dubiety. During the Second World War Durrell served the British government as agent and propagandist, and was a prominent figure among the varied assortment of non-combatants washed up in Alexandria until the Battle of El Alamein changed the fortunes of the Allies. There have been several books written about this period and some collections of poems and stories centring on the disjunct personalities who mingled in the besieged city – most notably the *Oasis* anthologies of wartime writing. Keith Douglas and Ian Fletcher were prominent among the poets. Alexandria was to serve Durrell more intensely after the war in his series of four novels set in the city, of which the first was *Justine*, an immediate success when published in 1957. But 'Alexandria' the poem is not like the novel. It is a dark rumination on human fate, a meditation on the dispersal of friends in wartime. He is not concerned primarily with the city of Cleopatra and the great age of Hellenism but with the modern cosmopolitan melting-pot, full of European and Levantine detritus cast on its shores. The 'you' in the poem's last lines is an unnamed lover, as so often in Durrell's poetry:

So we, learning to suffer and not condemn
Can only wish you this great pure wind
Condemned by Greece, and turning like a helm
Inland where it smokes the fires of men,
Spins weathercocks on farms or catches

The lovers in their quarrel in the sheets;
Or like a walker in the darkness might,
Knocks and disturbs the artist at his papers
Up there alone, upon the alps of night.

Here is a perfect picture of Durrell the bisected man – a lover of the East and its mysteries, but also a Northern European artist who will never escape the disciplined call to work at the rational art of poetry, 'alone, upon the alps of night'.

Although never truly at home back in Britain, Durrell was happy to serve the British Foreign Office in many different overseas roles. He was at times a cultural officer and a diplomat, and wrote several successful books about the diplomatic service. He wrote prose for money all his life, so that the three hundred pages of his poetry take up only a small space in the total body of his writing. His life's work does not give rise to the quandary expressed by T. S. Eliot about Thomas Hardy. Eliot accused Hardy of being a novelist who strayed into poetry, forgetting that Hardy had begun as a poet and took up novel-writing to earn a living. Durrell too started with poetry and lessened his commitment to it only in the fourth quarter of his life, but there was never any quarrel between his poetic and his fictional selves. The poetry leaked into the fiction and for many of his readers, such as myself, it is as a poet that we find him most admirable.

His humorous books of diplomatic life, *Esprit de Corps* and *Stiff Upper Lip*, spring from another of his facets, his expertise in light verse. Generations of readers have delighted in 'A Ballad of the Good Lord Nelson', an example of that hard-to-get-right genre, good not-so-clean-fun. Equally satirical are his playful expeditions into jargon and ideological language, especially 'Pressmarked Urgent', composed in telegraphese, and 'Two Poems in Basic English'. Despite his manifest loyalty to France and the Mediterranean, it is in his use of English forms and metres that he demonstrates his alliegance to English poetic traditions.

More than his novels, his travel books and studies of life in the islands of the Mediterranean are a source of the refinements of his verse. The best of these is *Prospero's Cell*, 'A Guide to the landscape and Manners of the Island of Coryra' (more familiar to most as Corfu), and the least convincing *Sicilian Carousel*. Durrell's heart remained in the Eastern reaches of Southern Europe and his travel symposia include studies of Cyprus (*Bitter Lemons*) and Rhodes (*Reflections on a Marine Venus*).

A compiler of the best of Durrell's poetry must face the charge mentioned earlier of his turning away to fiction. The two assemblies of novels gathered under the headings *The Alexandria Quartet* and *The Avignon Quintet* have been successes with the public and, to a lesser extent, with critics. Durrell's supporters have remonstrated with his chief deniers in Britain, rebuking them as dull stay-at-homes and inverted snobs. It should be kept in mind that when *Justine* and its three sequels of life in Alexandria appeared Britain was entering the decade of the Angry Young Men; poetry was witnessing the ascension of the Movement, and a little later of a taste for shamanistic and galvanic writing (Ted Hughes especially). Durrell's loyalties are very different from these. However, it is not my intention to emphasize the warring orthodoxies of poetic style. The twentieth century offers a long procession of talented artists working within modes sometimes experimental and sometimes traditional. I recall sharply my own first encounter with Durrell's poetry. I had bought that admirable anthology *The Penguin Book of Contemporary Verse*, edited by Kenneth Allott, in the year it appeared, 1950. Reading

Durrell was an eye-opener to me. An affection gained then has never dissipated. I return to his poetry month by month. The man who wrote the voluptuous fiction possessed a sharp and strongly poetic mind. The asperity of his verse makes it wear better.

Aspects of *The Alexandria Quartet* do emerge in the later poetry. 'Eight Aspects of Melissa', of which I have included three sections, are re-runs for *Justine* and *Clea* as well as recalling the story of Melissa, the virtuous maga of Ariosto's *Orlando Furioso*, so wonderfully represented in the Borghese Gallery, Rome, by the Ferrarese painter Dosso Dossi. 'A Persian Lady' is a slightly later poem also redolent of Durrell's Cavafy-like heat-hazes:

> He noted the perfected darkness of her beauty,
> The mind recoiling from a branding-iron:
> The sea advancing and retiring at her lacquered toes;
> How would one say 'to enflame' in her tongue,
> He wondered, knowing it applied to female beauty?
> When their eyes met he felt dis-figured
> It would have been simple – three paces apart!

Nearby this poem is 'Pursewarden's Incorrigibilia', on off-print of the Alexandria sequence. In 'Portfolio' he reactivates his tracing of an affair through the medium of literary commentary, as he had done in the Loeb Horace poem:

> And poetry, you once said, can be a deliverance
> And true in many sorts of different sense,
> Explicit or else like that awkward stare,
> The perfect form of public reticence.

He even anticipates the 'Martian' manner of Craig Raine in 'Vaumort':

One careless cemetery buzzes on and on
As if her tombstones were all hives
Overturned by the impatient dead –
We imagined they had stored up
The honey of their immortality
In the soft commotion the black bees make.

Below us, far away, the road to Paris.
You pour some wine upon a tomb.
The bees drink with us, the dead approve.

Lawrence Durrell died in 1990, and the last poem in *Collected* is dated 1980 but also listed as a revision of one written in 1974. He did not have a late Yeatsian flowering, but neither did he renegue on the brilliance of his precocious early work. He simply changed direction. A bookshop proprietor told me recently that he did a brisk trade in Durrell novels, but hardly seemed to know that their author was a poet. Not just a poet, I suggested, but one of the best of the past hundred years. And one of the most enjoyable. His special gift is the appropriateness with which he builds lyrical afflatus into aspects of reality. His poetry is not audacious technically though always beautiful as sound and syntax. Its innovation lies in its refusal to be more high-minded than the things it records, together with its handling of the whole lexicon of language. Already the Mediterranean he knew has changed from the mise-en-scène of his poems; one eternal symbol will never alter – the olive tree and its fruit, true symbols of place and genius. He put them into his writings of all kinds, and especially in one poem, 'Olives':

So the poets confused your attributes,
Said you were The Other but also the domestic useful,
And as the afflatus thrives on special discontents,

Little remedial trespasses of the heart, say,
Which grows it up: poor heart, starved pet of the mind:
They supposed your serenity compassed the human span,
Momentous, deathless, a freedom from the chain,
And every one wished they were like you,
Who live or dead brought solace,
The gold spunk of your berries making children fat.
Nothing in you being lame or fraudulent
You discountenanced all who saw you.

SELECTED POEMS OF
LAWRENCE DURRELL

Finis

There is a great heart-break in an evening sea;
Remoteness in the sudden naked shafts
Of light that die, tremulous, quivering
Into cool ripples of blue and silver . . .
So it is with these songs:
                              the ink has dried,
And found its own perpetual circuit here,
Cast its own net
Of little, formless mimicry around itself.
And you must turn away, smile . . .
                                    and forget.

The Death of General Uncebunke:
A Biography in Little
(1938)
To Kay in Tahiti: now dead

'Not satire but an exercise in ironic compassion, celebrating a simplicity of heart which is proof against superiority or the tooth of the dog . . . After all, we may have had other criteria, but they were only criteria.'

The Argument

General Uncebunke, named Konrad after his famous ancestor the medieval schoolman (*see epistolæ obscurorum virorum*), was born in 1880, and baptised in the same year at the village church, Uncebunke, Devon, England. On leaving Oxford he served with distinction in two wars.

In the intervals he travelled extensively in Peru, Siberia, Tibet, and Baffin Land and wrote many travel books of which *Roughing It in Tibet* is the best known to-day.

In 1925 he came home from his travels for good and settled down to country life in England, becoming Tory M.P. for Uncebunke, and increasing his literary reputation by his books of nature essays.

In 1930, owing to the death of his only daughter, he suffered from a temporary derangement of his mind and published that extraordinary volume of memoirs known as *Spernere Mundum*. He remained Tory member for Uncebunke, however, until his death on 2 April 1937.

He was laid in state for three days in the family vault; and the body was finally cremated according to his wish. His widow who survived him but three months is said to have scattered his ashes in the Channel as a tribute to a very gallant explorer and noble man.

[4]

Author's Note

You must know that this is one organic whole and must be read like a novel to be really appreciated. Also it is quite serious and should be read with the inner voice, preferably in some dialect.

I

My uncle sleeps in the image of death.
In the greenhouse and in the potting-shed
The wrens junket: the old girl with the trowel
Is a pillar of salt, insufferably brittle.
His not to reason why, though a thinking man.
Beside his mesmeric incomprehension
The little mouse mopping and mowing,
The giraffe and the spin-turtle, these can
On my picture-book look insufferably little
But knowing, incredibly Knowing.

II

My uncle has gone beyond astronomy.
He sleeps in the music-room of the Host.
Voyage was always his entertainment
Who followed a crooked needle under Orion,
Saw the griffin, left notes on the baobab,
Charted the Yellow Coast.

He like a faultless liner, finer never took air,
But snow on the wings altered the altitude,
She paused in a hollow pocket, faltered:
The enormous lighted bird is dashed in snow.

[5]

Now in the labyrinth God will put him wise,
Correct the instruments, will alter even
The impetuous stance, the focus of the eyes.

III

Aunt Prudence, she was the eye of the needle.
Sleeping, a shepherdess of ghostly sheep.
'Thy will be done in Baden Baden.
In Ouchy, Lord, and in Vichy.'
In the garden of the vicarage sorting stamps
Was given merit of the poor in spirit
For dusting a cinquefoil, tuning the little lamps.

Well, God sends weather, the English apple,
The weeping willow.
Grum lies the consort of Prudence quite:
Mum as a long fiddle in regimentals:
This sudden IT between two tropical thumbs.
Unwrinkle him, Lord, unriddle this strange gorgon,
For tall Prudence who softens the small lamps,
Gives humble air to the organ that it hums.

IV

My uncle sleeps in the image of death.
Not a bad sport the boys will tell you,
More than a spartan in tartan.
Yet he, fearing neither God nor man,
Feared suffocation by marble,
Wrote a will in hexameters, burnt the cakes,
Came through with the cavalry, ladies from hell,
Feared neither God nor man,
Devoted to the polo-pony, mesmerized by stamps.

[6]

Now in the stable the hypnotic horse-flesh
Champ, stamp, yawn, paw in the straw,
And in the bedroom the blind warhorse
Gallops all night the dark fields of Dis.

V

My uncle has gone beyond astronomy.
His sleep is of the Babylonian deep-sea
Darker than bitumen, defter than devil's alliances.
He has seen Golgotha in carnival:
Now in the shin-bone the smart worm
Presides at the death of the sciences,
The Trinity sleeps in his knee.

Curse Orion who pins my man like moth,
Who sleeps in the monotony of his zone,
Who is a daft ankle-bone among stars,
O shame on the beggar by silent lands
Who has nothing but carbon for his own.
Uncouple the flutes! Strike with the black rod!
Our song is no more plural, the bones
Are hollow without your air, Lord God.
Give us the language of diamonds or
The speech of the little stones.

VI

Prudence shall cross also the great white barrier.
God shall fold finally up the great fan —
Benevolent wings wheeling over the rectory,
The vicar, the thatcher, the rat-catcher,
Sure in this medicine help her all they can.
O she is sure in step with the step of the Master.

[7]

Winter loosens the apple, fastens the Eskimo.
Wearing his pug-marks for slippers shall follow,
Holding to common prayer, the Great Bear;
Over the Poles, wherever his voyages go.

Shall navigate also the great circle,
Confer with the serious mammoth, the sabre-tooth,
Come to the sole goal, palace of higher things,
Where God's good silverware spills on all faces,
And hazardously the good wizard, gives wings.

VII

My uncle sleeps in the image of death.
He sleeps the steep sleep of his zone,
His downward tilting sleep beyond alarm.
Heu! he will come to harm so alone.
Who says for him the things he dare not say?
He cannot speak to angels from his rock.
This pediment of sleep is his impediment.
Grant him the speech of sleep,
Not this dank slag, the deathward sediment.
Strike with the rod, Lord God.
Here was a ruddy bareback man,
Emptied his blood upon the frozen lake,
Wheeled back the screaming mares,
Crossing the Jordan.

Excuse me, Lord God, numberer of hairs,
Sender of telegrams, the poisoned arrow,
Suffer your faithful hound, give him
At least the portion of the common sparrow.

My uncle has gone beyond astronomy.
Three, six, nine of the dead languages
Are folded under his lip.
He has crossed over into Tartary,
Burnt his boats, dragged the black ice for bodies,
Seen trees in the water, skippered God's little ship.

He is now luggage, excess baggage,
Not wanted on voyage, scaling a pass,
Or swinging a cutlass in the Caribbean,
Under Barbados chewing the frantic marsh-rice,
Seven dead men, a crooked foot, a cracked jaw,
Ten teeth like hollow dice.

My uncle is sleeping in economy.
No word is wasted for the common ghost
Speaks inwards: he lies in the status
Of death's dumb music, the dumb dead king
On an ivory coast.

IX

Prudence had no dog and but one cat,
Black of bonnet the Lord's plain precept saw
At the at-home, on Calvary, in the darkest nook
He was there; He leaned on a window smiling,
The God Shepherd crooking his ghostly crook.
Prudence did dip and delve in the Holy Book,
Alpha to omega angels told her the tale,
Feeding the parrot, pensive over a croquet-hoop:

'Once upon a time was boy and girl,
Living on cherry, berry, fisherman's silver catch.

Now the crass cock crows in the coop,
Prudence, the door dangles, lacking a latch.'

X

My uncle has gone beyond astronomy.
He sleeps the sharp sleep of the unstrung harp.
Crossed into Tartary, he lies deep
In the flora and fauna of death,
Under a black snowline sleeps the steep,
Botanical, plant-pure sleep.

The soul is folded like a little mouse.
Body is mortuary here, the clock
Foiled in its own wheels – but he may be sleeping,
Even if no toe moves no where, the sock
Be empty of all but vessels – where is he creeping?
Where is my man's address? How does he perish
Who was my relish, who was without fault?

Strike with the black rod, Lord God.
This is the marmoreal person, the rocky one.
This is the pillar of savourless salt.

XI

My uncle has gone beyond astronomy.
He sleeps in the pocket of Lapland,
Hears thunder on a Monday, has known
Bone burn to ash for the urn's hold.
He has fine nails of his finger and of his toe.
Now colder than spittle is his mettle. The hand
Is cold bone touching cold stone. So
In the sad womb he plays the trump of doom.

[10]

Lord, here is music. This fine white 'cello
Hums no more to the gust of your air.
This supercilious fellow, think what was given
To nourish his engine, salt barley and beer.
All wasted, gone over, destroyed by death's leaven,
Scent of the apple and stain of the berry.
Now only the ignorant hedgehog dare,
Smelling the fruit in him, dance and be merry.

XII

Prudence was told the tale of the chimney-corner
In the ingle beetled over the red troll's book
Ate the white lie: 'Happily ever after,
A hunchback, a thimble, a smart swan,
Ride time's tall wave, musically on and on . . .'
Was it of God to bait and wait with the hook?
Was it of him black laughter at 'happily ever after',
A grass widow, a shadow embalmed in a story-book?

Memory is morsels offered of sparrows.
First prize a jug and bowl for correcting the clock,
Sending a telegram, gathering holy campion.
Lowly Prue is glum of finger and thumb,
Toe in the ember, dismembering spools of knitting.
Patience on a monument, passion on a cushion.
God's champion darning a sock, sitting.

XIII

My uncle sleeps in the image of death.
The shadow of other worlds, deep-water penumbra
Covers his marble: he is past sighing,
Body a great slug there, a fine white

Pike in a green pond lying.
My uncle was a red man. The dead man
Knew to shoe horses: the habits of the owl,
Time of tillage, foison, cutting of lumber,
Like Saint Columba,
Could coax the squirrels into his cowl.

Heu! for the tombeau, the sombre flambeau,
Immanent with God he lies in Limbo.
Break punic rock. Weather-man of the tomb,
We are left among little mice and insects,
Time's clock-work womb.

XIV

Prudence sweetly sang both crotchet and quaver,
Death riped an eyeball, the dog-days
Proffered salt without savour, the cards were cut.
She heard a primordial music, the Host's tune
For the guest's swoon – God going the gamut.
Honour a toast for the regimental mascot,
The thin girl, the boys of the blue fourteenth,
Driving to Ascot: a wedding under the sabres,
Tinker and tailorman, soldier or sailor,
Lads of the village entering harbour,
O respect also those windowless features,
The stainless face of the provincial barber.
Prudence plays monumental patience by candles:
The puffins sit in a book: the muffins are molten:
The crass clock chimes,
Timely the hour and deserved.
Presently will come the two welcome angels
Noise in the hall, the last supper be served.

The Hanged Man

From this glass gallows in famous entertainment,
Upside down and by the dust yellowed,
The hanged man considers a green county,
Hallowed by gallows on a high hill.

The rooks of his two blue eyes eating
A mineral diet, that smile not while
The invaders move: on the dark down there
Owls with soft scissors cherish him.

Yellower than plantains by the dust touched
These hands in their chamber-music turning,
As viol or cello, these might easily be
The sullen fingers of a fallen Charles.

So will the horseman speculate in his cloak,
The felloes of the wagon cease their screech,
While one widens the eye of the farm-girl
Telling how rope ripens on a high hill.

Father Nicholas His Death: Corfu
(1939)

Hush the old bones their vegetable sleep,
For the islands will never grow old.
Nor like Atlantis on a Monday tumble,
Struck like soft gongs in the amazing blue.

Dip the skull's chinks in lichens and sleep,
Old man, beside the water-gentry.
The hero standing knee-deep in his dreams
Will find and bind the name upon his atlas,
And put beside it only an X marked spot.

Leave memory to the two tall sons and lie
Calmed in smiles by the elegiac blue.
A man's address to God is the skeleton's humour,
A music sipped by the flowers.

Consider please the continuous nature of Love:
How one man dying and another smiling
Conserve for the maggot only a seed of pity,
As in winter's taciturn womb we see already
A small and woollen lamb on a hilltop hopping.

The dying and the becoming are one thing,
So wherever you go the musical always is;
Now what are your pains to the Great Danube's pains,
Your pyramids of despair against Ithaca
Or the underground rivers of Dis?

Your innocence shall be as the clear cistern
Where the lone animal in these odourless waters
Quaffs at his own reflection a shining ink.

Here at your green pasture the old psalms
Shall kneel like humble brutes and drink.

Hush then the finger bones their mineral doze
For the islands will never be old or cold
Nor ever the less blue: for the egg of beauty
Blossoms in new migrations, the whale's grey acres,
For men of the labyrinth of the dream of death.
So sleep.
All these warm when the flesh is cold.
And the blue will keep.

Nemea
(1940)

A song in the valley of Nemea:
Sing quiet, quite quiet here.

Song for the brides of Argos
Combing the swarms of golden hair:
Quite quiet, quiet there.

Under the rolling comb of grass,
The sword outrusts the golden helm.

Agamemnon under tumulus serene
Outsmiles the jury of skeletons:
Cool under cumulus the lion queen:

Only the drum can celebrate,
Only the adjective outlive them.

A song in the valley of Nemea:
Sing quiet, quiet, quiet here.

Tone of the frog in the empty well,
Drone of the bald bee on the cold skull,

Quiet, Quiet, Quiet.

At Epidaurus

The islands which whisper to the ambitious,
Washed all winter by the surviving stars
Are here hardly recalled: or only as
Stone choirs for the sea-bird,
Stone chairs for the statues of fishermen.
This civilized valley was dedicated to
The cult of the circle, the contemplation
And correction of famous maladies
Which the repeating flesh has bred in us also
By a continuous babyhood, like the worm in meat.

The only disorder is in what we bring here:
Cars drifting like leaves over the glades,
The penetration of clocks striking in London.
The composure of dolls and fanatics,
Financed migrations to the oldest sources:
A theatre where redemption was enacted,
Repentance won, the stones heavy with dew.
The olive signs the hill, signifying revival,
And the swallow's cot in the ruin seems how
Small yet defiant an exaggeration of love!

Here we can carry our own small deaths
With the resignation of place and identity;
A temple set severely like a dice
In the vale's Vergilian shade; once apparently
Ruled from the whitest light of the summer:
A formula for marble when the clouds
Troubled the architect, and the hill spoke
Volumes of thunder, the sibyllic god wept.
Here we are safe from everything but ourselves,
The dying leaves and the reports of love.

The land's lie, held safe from the sea,
Encourages the austerity of the grass chambers,
Provides a context understandably natural
For men who could divulge the forms of gods.
Here the mathematician entered his own problem,
A house built round his identity,
Round the fond yet mysterious seasons
Of green grass, the teaching of summer-astronomy.
Here the lover made his calculations by ferns,
And the hum of the chorus enchanted.
We, like the winter, are only visitors,
To prosper here the breathing grass,

Encouraging petals on a terrace, disturbing
Nothing, enduring the sun like girls
In a town window. The earth's flowers
Blow here original with every spring,
Shines in the rising of a man's age
Into cold texts and precedents for time.
Everything is a slave to the ancestor, the order
Of old captains who sleep in the hill.

Then smile, my dear, above the holy wands,
Make the indefinite gesture of the hands,
Unlocking this world which is not our world.
The somnambulists walk again in the north
With the long black rifles, to bring us answers.
Useless a morality for slaves: useless
The shouting at echoes to silence them.
Most useless inhabitants of the kind blue air,
Four ragged travellers in Homer.
All causes end within the great Because.

On Ithaca Standing
(1937)

Tread softly, for here you stand
On miracle ground, boy.
A breath would cloud this water of glass,
Honey, bush, berry and swallow.
This rock, then, is more pastoral, than
Arcadia is, Illyria was.

Here the cold spring lilts on sand.
The temperature of the toad
Swallowing under a stone whispers: 'Diamonds,
Boy, diamonds, and juice of minerals!'
Be a saint here, dig for foxes, and water,
Mere water springs in the bones of the hands.

Turn from the hearth of the hero. Think:
Other men have their emblems, I this:
The heart's dark anvil and the crucifix
Are one, have hammered and shall hammer
A nail of flesh, me to an island cross,
Where the kestrel's arrow falls only,
The green sea licks.

A Ballad of the Good Lord Nelson

The Good Lord Nelson had a swollen gland,
Little of the scripture did he understand
Till a woman led him to the promised land
   Aboard the Victory, Victory O.

Adam and Evil and a bushel of figs
Meant nothing to Nelson who was keeping pigs,
Till a woman showed him the various rigs
   Aboard the Victory, Victory O.

His heart was softer than a new laid egg,
Too poor for loving and ashamed to beg,
Till Nelson was taken by the Dancing Leg
   Aboard the Victory, Victory O.

Now he up and did up his little tin trunk
And he took to the ocean on his English junk,
Turning like the hour-glass in his lonely bunk
   Aboard the Victory, Victory O.

The Frenchman saw him a-coming there
With the one-piece eye and the valentine hair,
With the safety-pin sleeve and occupied air
   Aboard the Victory, Victory O.

Now you all remember the message he sent
As an answer to Hamilton's discontent –
There were questions asked about it in Parliament
   Aboard the Victory, Victory O.

Now the blacker the berry, the thicker comes the juice.
Think of Good Lord Nelson and avoid self-abuse,

For the empty sleeve was no mere excuse
  Aboard the Victory, Victory O.

'England Expects' was the motto he gave
When he thought of little Emma out on Biscay's wave,
And remembered working on her like a galley-slave
  Aboard the Victory, Victory O.

On First Looking into Loeb's Horace

I found your Horace with the writing in it;
Out of time and context came upon
This lover of vines and slave to quietness,
Walking like a figure of smoke here, musing
Among his high and lovely Tuscan pines.

All the small-holder's ambitions, the yield
Of wine-bearing grape, pruning and drainage
Laid out by laws, almost like the austere
Shell of his verses – a pattern of Latin thrift;
Waiting so patiently in a library for
Autumn and the drying of the apples;
The betraying hour-glass and its deathward drift.

Surely the hard blue winterset
Must have conveyed a message to him –
The premonitions that the garden heard
Shrunk in its shirt of hair beneath the stars,
How rude and feeble a tenant was the self,
An Empire, the body with its members dying –
And unwhistling now the vanished Roman bird?

The fruit-trees dropping apples; he counted them;
The soft bounding fruit on leafy terraces,
And turned to the consoling winter rooms
Where, facing south, began the great prayer,
With his reed laid upon the margins
Of the dead, his stainless authors,
Upright, severe on an uncomfortable chair.

Here, where your clear hand marked up
'The hated cypress' I added 'Because it grew

On tombs, revealed his fear of autumn and the urns',
Depicting a solitary at an upper window
Revising metaphors for the winter sea: 'O
Dark head of storm-tossed curls'; or silently
Watching the North Star which like a fever burns
Away the envy and neglect of the common,
Shining on this terrace, lifting up in recreation
The sad heart of Horace who must have seen it only
As a metaphor for the self and its perfection –
A burning heart quite constant in its station.

Easy to be patient in the summer,
The light running like fishes among the leaves,
Easy in August with its cones of blue
Sky uninvaded from the north; but winter
With its bareness pared his words to points
Like stars, leaving them pure but very few.

He will not know how we discerned him, disregarding
The pose of sufficiency, the landed man,
Found a suffering limb on the great Latin tree
Whose roots live in the barbarian grammar we
Use, yet based in him, his mason's tongue;
Describing clearly a bachelor, sedentary,
With a fond weakness for bronze-age conversation,
Disguising a sense of failure in a hatred for the young,

Who built in the Sabine hills this forgery
Of completeness, an orchard with a view of Rome;
Who studiously developed his sense of death
Till it was all around him, walking at the circus,
At the baths, playing dominoes in a shop –
The escape from self-knowledge with its tragic
Imperatives: *Seek, suffer, endure*. The Roman
In him feared the Law and told him where to stop.

So perfect a disguise for one who had
Exhausted death in art – yet who could guess
You would discern the liar by a line,
The suffering hidden under gentleness
And add upon the flyleaf in your tall
Clear hand: 'Fat, human and unloved,
And held from loving by a sort of wall,
Laid down his books and lovers one by one,
Indifference and success had crowned them all.'

Mythology

All my favourite characters have been
Out of all pattern and proportion:
Some living in villas by railways,
Some like Katsimbalis heard but seldom seen,
And others in banks whose sunless hands
Moved like great rats on ledgers.

Tibble, Gondril, Purvis, the Duke of Puke,
Shatterblossom and Dude Bowdler
Who swelled up in Jaffa and became a tree:
Hollis who had wives killed under him like horses
And that man of destiny,

Ramon de Something who gave lectures
From an elephant, founded a society
To protect the inanimate against cruelty.
He gave asylum to aged chairs in his home,
Lampposts and crockery, everything that
Seemed to him suffering he took in
Without mockery.

The poetry was in the pity. No judgement
Disturbs people like these in their frames
O men of the Marmion class, sons of the free.

Pressmarked Urgent
'Mens sana in corpore sano' – Motto for Press Corps

DESPATCH ADGENERAL PUBLICS EXTHE WEST
PERPETUAL MOTION QUITE UNFINDING REST
ADVANCES ETRETREATS UPON ILLUSION
PREPARES NEW METAPHYSICS PERCONFUSION

PARA PERDISPOSITION ADNEW EVIL
ETREFUSAL ADCONCEDE OUR ACTS ADDEVIL
NEITHER PROFIT SHOWS NOR LOSS
SEDSOME MORE PROPHETS NAILED ADCROSS

ATTACK IN FORCE SURMEANS NONENDS
BY MULTIPLYING CONFUSION TENDS
ADCLOUD THE ISSUES WHICH ARE PLAIN
COLON DISTINGUISH PROFIT EXGAIN

ETBY SMALL CONCEPTS LONG NEGLECTED
FIND VIRTUE SUBACTION CLEAR REFLECTED
ETWEIGHING THE QUANTUM OF THE SIN
BEGIN TO BE REPEAT BEGIN.

Two Poems in Basic English

I SHIPS. ISLANDS. TREES

These ships, these islands, these simple trees
Are our rewards in substance, being poor.
This earth a dictionary is
To the root and growth of seeing,
And to the servant heart a door.
Some on the green surface of the land
With all their canvas up in leaf and flower,
And some empty of influence
But from the water-winds,
Free as love's green attractions are.
Smoke bitter and blue from farms.
And points of feeble light in houses
Come after them in the scale
Of the material and the beautiful;
Are not less complex but less delicate
And less important than these living
Instruments of space,
Whose quiet communication is
With older trees in ships on the grey waves:
An order and a music
Like a writing on the skies
Too private for the reason or the pen;
Too simple even for the heart's surprise.

II NEAR EL ALAMEIN

This rough field of sudden war –
This sand going down to the sea, going down,
Was made without the approval of love,

By a general death in the desire for living.
Time got the range of impulse here:
On old houses with no thought of armies,
Burnt guns, maps and firing:
All the apparatus of man's behaviour
Put by in memories for books on history:
A growth like these bitter
Green bulbs in the hollow sand here.
But ideas and language do not go.
The rate of the simple things —
Men walking here, thinking of houses,
Gardens, or green mountains or beliefs:
Units of the dead in these living armies,
Making comparison of this bitter heat,
And the living sea, giving up its bodies,
Level and dirty in the mist,
Heavy with sponges and the common error.

from Eight Aspects of Melissa

II   CAIRO

Cut from the joints of this immense
Darkness upon the face of Egypt lying,
We move in the possession of our acts
Alone, the dread apostles of our weakness.

For look. The mauve street is swallowed
And the bats have begun to stitch slowly.
At the stable-door the carpenter's three sons
Bend over a bucket of burning shavings,
Warming their inwardness and quite unearthly
As the candle-marking time begins.

Three little magi under vast Capella,
Beloved of all as shy as the astronomer,
She troubles heaven with her golden tears,
Tears flowing down upon us at this window,
The children rapt, the mauve street swallowed,
The harps of flame among the shadows
In Egypt now and far from Nazareth.

V   PETRON, THE DESERT FATHER

Waterbirds sailing upon the darkness
Of Mareotis, this was the beginning:
Dry reeds touched by the shallow beaks he heard
On the sand trash of an estuary near Libya,
This dense yellow lake, ringing now
With the insupportable accents of the Word.

Common among the commoners of promise
He illustrated to the ordinary those
Who found no meaning in the flesh's weakness —
The elegant psychotics on their couches
In Alexandria, hardly tempted him,
With talk of business, war and lovely clothes.

The lemon-skinned, the gold, the half-aware
Were counters for equations he examined,
Grave as their statues fashioned from the life;
A pioneer in pleasure on the long
Linen-shaded colonnades he often heard
Girls' lips puff in the nostrils of the fife.

Now dense as clouded urine moved the lake
Whose waters were to be his ark and fort
By the harsh creed of water-fowl and snake,
To the wave-polished stone he laid his ear
And said: 'I dare not ask for what I hope,
And yet I may not speak of what I fear.'

VIII   A PROSPECT OF CHILDREN

All summer watch the children in the public garden,
The tribe of children wishing you were like them –
These gruesome little artists of the impulse
For whom the perfect anarchy sustains
A brilliant apprehension of the present,
In games of joy, of love or even murder
On this green springing grass will empty soon
A duller opiate, Loving, to the drains.

Cast down like asterisks among their toys,
Divided by the lines of daylight only
From adventure, crawl among the rocking-horses,

And the totems, dolls and animals and rings
To the tame suffix of a nursery sleep
Where all but few of them
The restless inventories of feeling keep.

Sleep has no walls. Sleep admits
The great Imago with its terror, yet they lie
Like something baking, candid cheek on finger,
With folded lip and eye
Each at the centre of the cobweb seeking
His boy or girl, begotten and confined
In terror like the edges of a table
Begot by passion and confirmed in error.

What can they tell the watcher at the window,
Writing letters, smoking up there alone,
Trapped in the same limitation of his growth
And yet not envying them their childhood
Since he endured his own?

Alexandria

To the lucky now who have lovers or friends,
Who move to their sweet undiscovered ends,
Or whom the great conspiracy deceives,
I wish these whirling autumn leaves:
Promontories splashed by the salty sea,
Groaned on in darkness by the tram
To horizons of love or good luck or more love –
As for me I now move
Through many negatives to what I am.

Here at the last cold Pharos between Greece
And all I love, the lights confide
A deeper darkness to the rubbing tide;
Doors shut, and we the living are locked inside
Between the shadows and the thoughts of peace:
And so in furnished rooms revise
The index of our lovers and our friends
From gestures possibly forgotten, but the ends
Of longings like unconnected nerves,
And in this quiet rehearsal of their acts
We dream of them and cherish them as Facts.

Now when the sea grows restless as a conscript,
Excited by fresh wind, climbs the sea-wall,
I walk by it and think about you all:
B. with his respect for the Object, and D.
Searching in sex like a great pantry for jars
Marked 'Plum and apple'; and the small, fell
Figure of Dorian ringing like a muffin-bell –
All indeed whom war or time threw up

On this littoral and tides could not move
Were objects for my study and my love.

And then turning where the last pale
Lighthouse, like a Samson blinded, stands
And turns its huge charred orbit on the sands
I think of you – indeed mostly of you,
In whom a writer would only name and lose
The dented boy's lip and the close
Archer's shoulders; but here to rediscover
By tides and faults of weather, by the rain
Which washes everything, the critic and the lover.

At the doors of Africa so many towns founded
Upon a parting could become Alexandria, like
The wife of Lot – a metaphor for tears;
And the queer student in his poky hot
Tenth floor room above the harbour hears
The sirens shaking the tree of his heart,
And shuts his books, while the most
Inexpressible longings like wounds unstitched
Stir in him some girl's unquiet ghost.

So we, learning to suffer and not condemn
Can only wish you this great pure wind
Condemned by Greece, and turning like a helm
Inland where it smokes the fires of men,
Spins weathercocks on farms or catches
The lovers at their quarrel in the sheets;
Or like a walker in the darkness might,
Knocks and disturbs the artist at his papers
Up there alone, upon the alps of night.

Poggio

The rubber penis, the wig, the false breasts . . .
The talent for entering rooms backwards
Upon a roar of laughter, with his dumb
Pained expression, wheeling there before him
That mythological great hippo's bum:

'Who should it be but Poggio?' The white face,
Comical, flat, and hairless as a cheese.
Nose like a member: something worn:
A Tuscan fig, a leather can, or else,
A phallus made of putty and slapped on.

How should you know that behind
All this the old buffoon concealed a fear –
And reasonable enough – that he might be
An artist after all? Always after this kind
Of side-splitting evening, sitting there
On a three-legged stool and writing, he

Hoped poems might form upon the paper.
But no. Dirty stories. The actress and the bishop.
The ape and the eunuch. This crapula clung
To him for many years between his dinners . . .
He sweated at them like a ham unhung.

And like the rest of us hoped for
The transfigured story or the mantic line
Of poetry free from this mortuary smell.
For years slept badly – who does not?
Took bribes, and drugs, ate far too much and dreamed.
Married unwisely, yes, but died quite well.

from Cities, Plains and People
(Beirut, 1943)

XVI

Small temptations now – to slumber and to sleep,
Where the lime-green, odourless
And pathless island waters
Crossing and uncrossing, partnerless
By hills alone and quite incurious
Their pastures of reflection keep.

For Prospero remains the evergreen
Cell by the margin of the sea and land,
Who many cities, plains, and people saw
Yet by his open door
In sunlight fell asleep
One summer with the Apple in his hand.

from Eternal Contemporaries: Six Portraits

III   BASIL THE HERMIT

Banished from the old roof-tree Patmos
Where the dynasts gathered honey,
Like dancing bears, with smoking rituals,
Or skimmed the fat of towns with levy-money,
Uncaring whether God or Paradise exist,
Laid up themselves estates in providence
While greed crouched in each hairy fist,

Basil, the troubled flower of scepticism,
Chose him a pelt, and a cairn of chilly stone,
Became the author of a famous schism:
A wick for oil, a knife, a broken stool
Were all, this side of hell, he dared to own.
For twenty years in Jesus went to school.

Often, looking up, he saw them there
As from some prism-stained pool:
Dark dots like birds along the battlements,
Old rooks swayed in a rotten tree.
They waved: he did not answer, although he
Felt kindly to them all, for they could do
What he could not: he did not dare to pray.
His inner prohibitions were a sea
On which he floated spellbound day by day.

World and its fevers howled outside: within
The Omen and the Fret that hemmed him in,
The sense of his complete unworthiness
Pressed each year slowly tighter like a tourniquet.

The Daily Mirror

Writing this stuff should not have been like
Suicide over some ordinary misapprehension:

A man going into his own house, say,
Turning out all the lights before undressing,

At the bedside of some lovely ignoramus
Whispering: 'Tomorrow I swear is the last time.'

Or: 'Believe, and I swear you will never die.'
This nib dragged out like the late train

Racing on iron bars for the north.
Target: another world, not necessarily better,

Of course, but different, completely different.
The hour-glass shifting its trash of seconds.

If it does not end this way perhaps some other.
Gossip lying in a furnished room, blinds drawn.

A poem with its throat cut from ear to ear.

from The Anecdotes

XV   IN RHODES

From the intellect's grosser denominations
I can sort one or two, how indistinctly,
Living on as if in some unripened faculty
Quite willing to release them, let them die.

Putative mothers-in-ideas like that Electra's
Tallow orphan skin in a bed smelling faintly
Of camphor, the world, the harsh laugh of Glauca:
But both like geometrical figures now,
Then musky, carmine . . . (I am hunting for
The precise shade of pink for Acte's mouth:
Pink as the sex of a mastiff . . .)

Now as the great paunch of this earth
Allows its punctuation by seeds, some to be
Trees, some men walking as trees, so the mind
Offers its cakes of spore to time in them:
The sumptuary pleasure-givers living on
In qualities as sure as taste of hair and mouth,
White partings of the hair like highways,
Permutations of a rose, buried beneath us now,
Under the skin of thinking like a gland
Discharging its obligations in something trivial:
Say a kiss, a handclasp: say a stone tear.

They went. We did not hear them leave.
They came. We were not ready for them.
Then turning the sphere to death
Which like some great banking corporation
Threatens, forecloses, and from all

Our poses selects the one sea-change –
Naturally one must smile to see him powerless
Not in the face of these small fictions
But in the greater one they nourished
By exhaustion of the surfaces of life,
Leaving the True Way, so that suddenly
We no longer haunted the streets
Of our native city, guilty as a popular singer,
Clad in the fur of some wild animal.

The Tree of Idleness

I shall die one day I suppose
In this old Turkish house I inhabit:
A ragged banana-leaf outside and here
On the sill in a jam-jar a rock-rose.

Perhaps a single pining mandolin
Throbs where cicadas have quarried
To the heart of all misgiving and there
Scratches on silence like a pet locked in.

Will I be more or less dead
Than the village in memory's dispersing
Springs, or in some cloud of witness see,
Looking back, the selfsame road ahead?

By the moist clay of a woman's wanting,
After the heart has stopped its fearful
Gnawing, will I descry between
This life and that another sort of haunting?

No: the card-players in tabs of shade
Will play on: the aerial springs
Hiss: in bed lying quiet under kisses
Without signature, with all my debts unpaid

I shall recall nights of squinting rain,
Like pig-iron on the hills: bruised
Landscapes of drumming cloud and everywhere
The lack of someone spreading like a stain.

Or where brown fingers in the darkness move,
Before the early shepherds have awoken,

Tap out on sleeping lips with these same
Worn typewriter keys a poem imploring

Silence of lips and minds which have not spoken.

Author's Note: The title of this poem is taken from the name of the tree
which stands outside Bellapaix Abbey in Cyprus, and which confers the gift
of pure idleness on all who sit under it.

A Portrait of Theodora

I recall her by a freckle of gold
In the pupil of one eye, an odd
Strawberry-gold: and after many years
Of forgetting that musical body –
Arms too long, wrists too slender –
Remember only the unstable wishes
Disquieting the flesh. I will not
Deny her pomp was laughable, urban:
Behind it one could hear the sad
Provincial laughter rotted by insomnia.

None of these meetings are planned,
I guess, or willed by the exemplars
Of a city's love – a city founded in
The name of love: to me is always
Brown face, white teeth, cheap summer frock
In green and white stripes and then
Forever a strawberry eye. I recalled no more
For years. The eye was lying in wait.

Then in another city from the same
Twice-used air and sheets, in the midst
Of a parting: the same dark bedroom,
Arctic chamber-pot and cruel iron bed,
I saw the street-lamp unpick Theodora
Like an old sweater, unwrinkle eyes and mouth,
Unbandaging her youth to let me see
The wounds I had not understood before.

How could I have ignored such wounds?
The bloody sweepings of a loving smile

Strewed like Osiris among the dunes?
Now only my experience recognizes her
Too late, among the other great survivors
Of the city's rage, and places her among
The champions of love – among the true elect!

A Persian Lady

Some diplomatic mission – no such thing as 'fate' –
Brought her to the city that ripening spring.
She was much pointed out – a Lady-in-Waiting –
To some Persian noble; well, and here she was
Merry and indolent amidst fashionable abundance.
By day under a saffron parasol on royal beaches,
By night in a queer crocketed tent with tassels.

He noted the perfected darkness of her beauty,
The mind recoiling as from a branding-iron:
The sea advancing and retiring at her lacquered toes;
How would one say 'to enflame' in her tongue,
He wondered, knowing it applied to female beauty?
When their eyes met he felt dis-figured
It would have been simple – three paces apart!

Disloyal time! They let the seminal instant go,
The code unbroken, the collision of ripening wishes
Abandoned to hiss on in the great syllabaries of memory.
Next day he deliberately left the musical city
To join a boring water-party on the lake.
Telling himself 'Say what you like about it,
I have been spared very much in this business.'

He meant, I think, that never should he now
Know the slow disgracing of her mind, the slow
Spiral of her beauty's deterioration, flagging desires,
The stagnant fury of the temporal yoke,
Grey temple, long slide into fat.

On the other hand neither would she build him sons
Or be a subject for verses – the famished in-bred poetry

Which was the fashion of his time and ours.
She would exist, pure, symmetrical and intact
Like the sterile hyphen which divides and joins
In a biography the year of birth and death.

Olives

The grave one is patron of a special sea,
Their symbol, food and common tool in one,
Yet chthonic as ever the ancients realized,
Noting your tips in trimmings kindled quick,
Your mauled roots roared with confused ardours,
Holding in heat, like great sorrows contained
By silence; dead branch or alive grew pelt
Refused the rain and harboured the ample oil
For lamps to light the human eye.

So the poets confused your attributes,
Said you were The Other but also the domestic useful,
And as the afflatus thrives on special discontents,
Little remedial trespasses of the heart, say,
Which grows it up: poor heart, starved pet of the mind:
They supposed your serenity compassed the human span,
Momentous, deathless, a freedom from the chain,
And every one wished they were like you,
Who live or dead brought solace,
The gold spunk of your berries making children fat.
Nothing in you being lame or fraudulent
You discountenanced all who saw you.

No need to add how turning downwind
You pierce again today the glands of memory,
Or how in summer calms you still stand still
In etchings of a tree-defining place.

Stone Honey

Reading him is to refresh all nature,
Where, newly elaborated, reality attends.
The primal innocence in things confronting
His eye as thoughtful, innocence as unstudied . . .
One could almost say holy in the scientific sense.
So while renewing nature he relives for us
The simple things our inattention staled,
Noting sagely how water can curl like hair,
Its undisciplined recoil moving mountains
Or drumming out geysers in the earth's crust,
Or the reflex stroke which buries ancient cities.

But water was only one of the things Leonardo
Was keen on, liked to sit down and draw.
It would not stay still; and sitting there beside
The plate of olives, the comb of stone honey,
Which seemed so eternal in the scale of values,
So philosophically immortal, he was touched
By the sense of time's fragility, the semen of fate.
The adventitious seconds, days or seasons,
Though time stood still some drowsy afternoon,
Became for him dense, gravid with their futurity.
Life was pitiless after all, advancing and recoiling
Like the seas of the mind. The only purchase was
This, deliberately to make the time to note:
'The earth is budged from its position by the
Merest weight of a little bird alighting on it.'

Portfolio

Late seventeenth, a timepiece rusted by dew,
Candles, a folio of sketches where rotting
I almost found you a precarious likeness –
The expert relish of the charcoal stare!
The copies, the deposits, why the very
Undermeaning and intermeaning of your mind,
Everything was there.

Your age too, its preoccupations like ours . . .
'The cause of death is love though death is all'
Or else: 'Freedom resides in choice yet choice
Is only a fatal imprisonment among the opposites.'
Who told you you were free? What can it mean?
Come, drink! The simple kodak of the hangman's brain
Outstares us as it once outstared your world.
After all, we were not forced to write,
Who bade us heed the inward monitor?

And poetry, you once said, can be a deliverance
And true in many sorts of different sense,
Explicit or else like that awkward stare,
The perfect form of public reticence.

Envoi

Be silent, old frog.
Let God compound the issue as he must,
And dog eat dog
Unto the final desecration of man's dust.
The just will be devoured by the unjust.

Seferis

Time quietly compiling us like sheaves
Turns round one day, beckons the special few,
With one bird singing somewhere in the leaves,
Someone like K. or somebody like you,
Free-falling target for the envious thrust,
So tilting into darkness go we must.

Thus the fading writer signing off
Sees in the vast perspectives of dispersal
His words float off like tiny seeds,
Wind-borne or bird-distributed notes,
To the very end of loves without rehearsal,
The stinging image riper than his deeds.

Yours must have set out like ancient
Colonists, from Delos or from Rhodes,
To dare the sun-gods, found great entrepôts,
Naples or Rio, far from man's known abodes,
To confer the quaint Grecian script on other men;
A new Greek fire ignited by your pen.

How marvellous to have done it and then left
It in the lost property office of the loving mind,
The secret whisper those who listen find.
You show us all the way the great ones went,
In silences becalmed, so well they knew
That even to die is somehow to invent.

from Solange

The dreams of Solange confused no issues, solved no problems, for on the auto-screen among our faces appeared always and most often others like Papillon the tramp, a childhood scarecrow built of thorns. He turned the passive albums of her sleep with long fingers, one of them a steel hook. Papillon represented a confederacy of buried impulses which could resurrect among the tangled sheet, a world of obscure resentments, fine and brutal as lace, the wedding-cake lying under its elaborate pastry. His ancient visions sited in that crocodile-mask fired her. And such dreams as he recounted revived among her own – Paris as some huge penis sliced up and served around a whole restaurant by masked waiters. And the lovers murmuring 'I love you so much I could eat you'. She takes up knife and fork and begins to eat. The screams might awake her, bathed in sweat, to hear the real face of Marc the underwriter saying something like: 'All our ills come from incautious dreaming.' There were so many people in the world, how to count them all? Perhaps causality was a way of uniting god with laughter? Solange avec son œil luisant et avide, holding a handbag full of unposted cards.

Add to the faces the Japanese student whose halting English was full of felicities only one could notice; as when 'Lord Byron committed incense with his sister, and afterwards took refuse in the church'. He too for a season cast a spell. Then one day he recited a poem which met with her disfavour.

> She was eighteen but already god-avowed,
> She sought out the old philosopher
> Expressly to couple with him, so to be

Bathed in the spray of his sperm
The pneuma of his inner idea.
Pleasure and instruction were hers,
She corrected her course by his visions.
But of all this a child was born,
But in him, not in her, as a poem
With as many legs as a spider
In a web the size of a world.

Then Deutre, the latest of our company
Who believed all knowledge to be founded
Deep in the orgasm, rising into emphasis
As individual consciousness, the know-thyself,
Bit by bit, with checks and halts, but always
By successive amnesias dragged into conception,
A school of pneuma for the inward eye
Reflecting rays which pass in deliberate tangence
To the ordinary waking sense, focuses the heart.
Patiently must Solange pan for male gold
White legs spread like geometer's compasses
Over her native city. The milk-teeth fall at last.
Gradually the fangs develop, breathing changes,
And out of the tapestry of monkey grimaces
Born of no diagrams no act of will
But simple subservience to a natural law, He comes,
He emerges, He is there. Who? I do not know.
Deutre presumably in the guise of Rilke's angel
Or Balzac's double mirrored androgyne.
Deutre makes up his lips at dusk,
His sputum is tinged with venous blood.
Nevertheless a purity of intent is established
Simple as on its axis spins an earth.
It was his pleasure to recite

With an emphasis worthy of the Vedas
Passages from the Analysis Situs: as
        la géometrie à n dimensions
        a un objet réel, personne n'en
        doute aujourd'hui. Les Etres
        de l'hyperespace sont susceptibles
        de définitions précises comme ceux
        de l'espace ordinaire, et si nous
        ne pouvons les répresenter nous
        pouvons les concevoir et les étudier.

The third eye belongs to spatial consciousness
He seems to say; there is a way of growing.
It was he who persuaded me at Christmas to go away.
Far southwards to submit myself to other towns
To landscapes more infernal and less purifying.
He persuaded Solange to lend me the money and she
Was glad to repay what the acrobat had spent,
But she saw no point in it, 'Who can live outside
Paris, among barbarians, and to what end?
Besides all these places are full of bugs
And you can see them on the cinema without moving
For just a few francs, within reach of a café.
But if go you must I will see you off.'

Remoter than Aldebaran, Deutre smiled.
Only many years later was I able
To repay him with such words as:
'Throughout the living world as we know it
The genetic code is based on four letters,
The Pythagorean Quarternary, as you might say.'
He did not even smile, for he was dying.
Man's achievement of a bipedal gait has freed
His hands for tools, weapons and the embrace.

the days will be lengthening
into centuries, Solange
and neither witness will be there,
seek no comparisons among
dolls' houses of the rational mind
coevals don't compare
a gesture broken off by dusk
heartless as boredom is or hope
blood seeks the soil it has to soak
in the fulfilment of a scope
fibres of consciousness will grow
lavish as any coffin load
and every touching entity
the puritan grave will swallow up
the silences will atrophy.

So we came, riding through the soft lithograph
Of Paris in the rain, the spires
Empting their light, the mercury falling,
Streets draining into the sewers,
The yokel clockface of the Gare de Lyon
On a warehouse wall the word 'Imputrescible'
Then slowly night: but suddenly
The station was full of special trains,
Long hospital trains with red crosses
Drawn blinds, uniformed nurses, doctors.
Dimly as fish in tanks moved pyjama-clad figures
Severed from the world, one would have said
Fresh from catastrophe, a great battlefield.
'O well the war has come' she said with resignation.
But it was only the annual pilgrimage to Lourdes,
The crippled the lame the insane the halt
All heading southwards towards the hopeless miracle.

Each one felt himself the outside chance,
Thousands of sick outsiders.
A barrel organ played a rotting waltz.
The Government was determined to root out gambling.
My path was not this one; but it equally needed
A sense of goodbye. Firm handclasp of hard little paw,
The clasp of faithful business associates, and
'When you come back, you know where to find me.'
                    four steps up
                    four steps down
                    the station ramp eludes
                    the mangy town
                    the temporary visa
                    with the scarlet stamp
                    flowers of soda
                    shower the quays
                    engines piss hot spume
                    giants in labour
                    drip and sweat like these
                    slam the carriage door
                    only this and nothing more.

I write these lines towards dusk
On the other side of the world,
A country with stranger inhabitants,
Chestnut candles, fevers, and white water.
Such small perplexities as vex the mind,
Solange, became for writers precious to growth,
But the fluttering sails disarm them,
Wet petals sticking to a sky born nude.
The magnitudes, insights, fears and proofs
Were your unconscious gift. They still weigh
With the weight of Paris forever hanging

White throat wearing icy gems,
A parody of stars as yet undiscovered.
Here they tell me I have come to terms.
But supposing I had chosen to march on you
Instead of on such a star – what then?
Instead of this incubus of infinite duration,
I mean to say, whose single glance
Brings loving to its knees?
Yes, wherever the ant-hills empty
Swarm the fecund associations, crossing
And recrossing the sky-pathways of sleep.
We labour only to be relatively
Sincere as ants perhaps are sincere.
Yet always the absolute vision must keep
The healthy lodestar of its stake in love.
You'll see somewhere always the crystal body
Transparent, held high against the light
Blaze like a diamond in the deep.
How can a love of life be ever indiscreet
For even in that far dispersing city today
Ants must turn over in their sleep.

Pursewarden's Incorrigibilia

It will be some time before the Pursewarden papers and manuscripts are definitively sorted and suitably edited; but a few of his *boutades* have turned up in the papers of his friends. Here are two examples of what someone called his 'incorrigibilia'; he himself referred to them as Authorised Versions. The first, which was sung to the melody of *Deutschland, Deutschland Uber Alles*, in a low nasal monotone, generally while he was shaving, went as follows:

> Take me back where sex is furtive
> And the midnight copper roams;
> Where instead of comfy brothels
> We have Lady Maud's At Homes.
> Pass me up that White Man's Burden
> Fardels of Democracy;
> Three faint cheers for early closing,
> Hip-Hip-Hip Hypocrisy!
> Sweet Philistia of my childhood
> Where our valiant churchmen pant:
> 'Highest standard of unliving,
> Longest five-day week of Cant.'
> Avert A.I.! Shun Vivisection!
> Join the RSPCA,
> Lead an anti-litter faction!
> Leave your leavings in a tray!
> Cable grandma I'll be ready,
> Waiting on the bloody dock;
> With a hansom for my luggage –
> Will the French release my cock?
> Take me back in An Appliance,

For I doubt if I can walk;
Back to art dressed in a jockstrap,
Back to a Third Programme Talk.
Roll me back down Piccadilly
Where our National Emblem stands,
Watching coppers copping tartlets,
Eros! wring thy ringless hands!
Ineffectual intellectual
Chewing of the Labour rag,
Take me back where every Cause
Is round the corner, in the bag.
Buy me then my steamer ticket
For the land for which I burn . . .
Yet, on second thoughts, best make it
The usual weekday cheap return!

(wr. 1962; pr. 1980)

[The second example, not printed here, is titled
'Frankie and Johnny, New Style']

Vaumort

For 'Buttons'

Seemingly upended in the sky,
Cloudless as minds asleep
One careless cemetery buzzes on and on
As if her tombstones were all hives
Overturned by the impatient dead –
We imagined they had stored up
The honey of their immortality
In the soft commotion the black bees make.

Below us, far away, the road to Paris.
You pour some wine upon a tomb.
The bees drink with us, the dead approve.

It is weeks ago now and we are back
In our burnt and dusty Languedoc,
Yet often in the noon-silences
I hear the Vaumort bees, taste the young wine,
Catch a smile hidden in sighs.

In the long grass you found a ring, remember?
A child's toy ring. Yes, I know that whenever
I want to be perfectly alone
With the memory of you, of that whole day
It's to Vaumort that I'll be turning.